Fashion Neckwear

By Lisa Gentry

Create 11 stylish looks with mesh & ribbon yarns!

Mesh Yarn 2

Making Ruffles 3

Making a Cord or Band 3

Ribbon Yarn 4

Working With Mesh & Ribbon Yarns 5

Basic Techniques 6

Finishing 9

LEISURE ARTS, INC.
Maumelle, Arkansas

FASHION YARNS

Fabulous mesh and ribbon yarns are the key element in these 11 impressive cowls, scarves, and neckwarmers. Pages 2-9 explain how to work with these specialty yarns, and bonus online videos are available for extra support wherever you see a camera icon.

MESH YARN

Novelty mesh yarns come in a wide array of styles. Some have a decorative border with a touch of metallic fiber or sequins. On some, the mesh loops are larger to allow extra drape.

There are two methods of working with mesh yarn. One method makes ruffled projects and the other method makes a thick cord or band. Both methods can be used in the same project to make flowers separated by cords or bands.

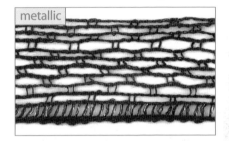
metallic

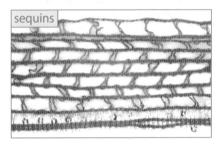
sequins

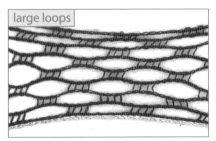
large loops

📹 MAKING RUFFLES

Stretch the yarn out so you can see all of the mesh, placing the mesh edge at the top and the solid edge at the bottom *(Fig. 1)*. You will crochet using the top row of mesh loops.

Fig. 1

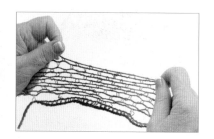

📹 MAKING A CORD OR BAND

The yarn is held as a single strand, without stretching it out *(Fig. 2)*. Chains are used to form a cord and single crochets are used to form a band.

Fig. 2

RIBBON YARN

Ribbon yarn is made up of a band of loosely woven threads. The top edge has large loops that resemble a ladder. Crochet into these loops.

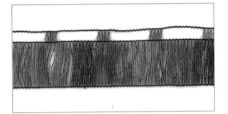

PREPARING RIBBON YARN

Ribbon yarn may come in a hank. Unfold the hank and remove the thread ties. Carefully and evenly wind the entire hank flat around an empty paper towel tube *(Fig. 3)*. Place a rubber band around the ribbon yarn on the tube to prevent it from unwrapping when not in use.

Fig. 3

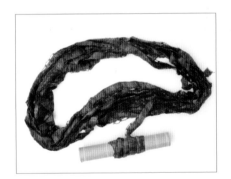

WORKING WITH MESH & RIBBON YARNS

To prevent the piece from accidentally unraveling when you are not working on your project, slip the loop from your hook onto a safety pin.

If there is a knot in the yarn, untie it or cut it out. Overlap both ends and continue working through both layers as if they were only one.

🎥 MARKERS

Split ring markers are used to help you see the stitches. They are placed in a chain or a single crochet after the stitch is made *(Fig. 4a)*. Remove the marker after the stitch is worked into. Once you understand where to work, it won't be necessary to use markers.

TIP: If you are not sure where to insert the marker, place it around both strands of the loop (under the hook) **before** the stitch is made *(Fig. 4b)*. The marker will be in the stitch after it is made.

Fig. 4b

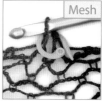

Fig. 4a

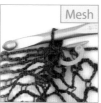

BASIC TECHNIQUES

GETTING STARTED

Always insert your hook in the loops from **front** to **back** *(Fig. 5)*.

Fig. 5

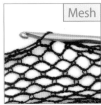

To begin a project, skip approximately 4 loops (or the number of loops indicated in the instructions) and insert your hook in the next loop. **This is equivalent to a slip knot.**

> **TIP:** When working with ribbon yarn, be careful to only pull the loop through the stitch or loop on hook, and not the band of woven threads.

CHAIN 1

Often when making a Foundation Chain, you will be instructed to skip a loop before working a chain as illustrated in Fig. 6. This is to space the chains apart. Only skip loops as indicated in the individual project.

▦◀ **To chain 1**, insert your hook in the next loop on the yarn and pull the loop through the loop on the hook *(Fig. 6)*.

Fig. 6

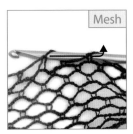

When working into the Foundation Chain *(Fig. 7a)*, work into both loops of the chains.

Fig. 7a

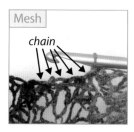

If you can't see where your chains are, especially when working with the mesh yarn, it may be helpful to place a marker *(see Markers, page 5)* in each chain as it is made *(Fig. 7b)*.

Fig. 7b

🎥 SC USING 2 LOOPS

Insert your hook in the next stitch on your project and in the next loop on the yarn, pull the loop through the stitch (2 loops on hook) *(Fig. 8a)*, insert your hook in the next loop on the yarn and pull the loop through both loops on the hook *(Fig. 8b)*.

Fig. 8a

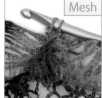

Fig. 8b

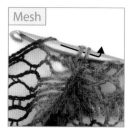

📹 SC USING 4 LOOPS

Insert your hook in the next stitch on your project, skip the next loop on the yarn, insert your hook in the next loop and pull the loop through the stitch *(Fig. 9a)* (2 loops on hook).

Fig. 9a

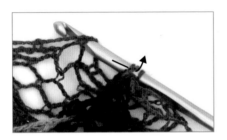

Skip the next loop on the yarn, insert your hook in the next loop and pull the loop through both loops on the hook *(Fig. 9b)*.

Fig. 9b

📹 SLIP STITCH

Insert your hook in the stitch on your project as indicated and in the next loop on the yarn, pull the loop through the stitch and the loop on the hook *(Fig. 10)*.

Fig. 10

FINISHING

RIBBON & MESH YARN

When ribbon or mesh yarn is used for a complete project or for an edging at the end of a project worked in medium weight yarn, there will be one loop left on your hook that will need to be secured. Carefully slip the loop off your hook and using a sewing needle and matching thread, sew the loop in place *(Fig. 11)*.

Fig. 11

The raw edge of the ribbon and mesh yarn ends will need to be hidden. This is why a short end approximately 3" to 4" (7.5 cm to 10 cm) long is left at each end.

There are many ways to hide the ends. The top edge of the end can be gathered or it can be folded twice to the inside; the corner can be folded up; or the short end can be tucked under the last ruffle. Using a sewing needle and matching thread, sew the end in place.

You can also use a large yarn needle and weave the ends into the ruffle.

MEDIUM WEIGHT YARN

Thread a yarn needle with the yarn end, then insert the needle under the stitches as indicated by the arrow *(Fig. 12)*, reversing the direction that you are weaving several times. Once the end is hidden, clip it close to the work.

Fig. 12

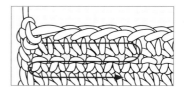

RUFFLE SCARF

 EASY

Finished Size: Approximately 4¹/₂" x 44" (11.5 cm x 112 cm) relaxed
Note: Please refer to Fashion Yarns, pages 2-9, and our online videos
for help with any techniques not familiar to you.

SHOPPING LIST

Yarn
(Mesh Super Bulky Weight)
[3.5 ounces, 30 yards
(100 grams, 27 meters)
per ball]:
☐ 1 ball

Crochet Hook
☐ Size H (5 mm)

Additional Supplies
☐ Sewing needle and
matching thread
☐ Split ring markers

Gauge is not important for this
project.

INSTRUCTIONS
When working a foundation
Chain, place a marker in the first
chain made *(Fig. 4a or 4b, page 5)*.
It may be helpful to also place a
marker in each chain as it is made.
This will help you see where
to insert your hook on Row 1
(Fig. 7b, page 7).

As you work, stretch the yarn out,
having the mesh edge at the top.
Work only in the top row of mesh
loops.

Foundation Chain: Skip first
8 loops from end and insert hook
in next loop, (skip next loop, ch 1)
5 times: 5 chs.

The model was made using
Red Heart® Boutique Sashay®, #1946 Ballet.

Work all sc using 4 loops
(Figs. 9a & b, page 8).

Remove marker as you work
into the marked stitch.

Row 1: Turn; skip first ch, sc
in next ch, place marker in
sc just made, sc in last 3 chs:
4 sc.

Row 2: Ch 1, turn; skip
turning ch just made, sc in
next sc, place marker in sc
just made, sc in last 3 sc.

Repeat Row 2 until there
are at least 8 top loops
remaining on the mesh yarn
after completing a row.

Trim the mesh yarn leaving
8 loops. Secure the loop on
hook and hide the raw edge
of the mesh yarn ends
(see Finishing, page 9).

RIBBON SCARF

■■□□ EASY

Shown on page 15.

Finished Size: Approximately 2¹/₂" x 43" (6.5 cm x 109 cm) relaxed

Note: Please refer to Fashion Yarns, pages 2-9, and our online videos for help with any techniques not familiar to you.

SHOPPING LIST

Yarn
(Ribbon Super Bulky Weight)
[3.5 ounces, 42 yards
(100 grams, 38 meters)
per hank]:

**SUPER BULKY
6**

☐ 1 hank

Crochet Hook
☐ Size H (5 mm)

Additional Supplies
☐ Sewing needle and
matching thread
☐ Split ring markers

Gauge is not important for this project.

INSTRUCTIONS

When working a Foundation Chain, place a marker in the first chain made *(Fig. 4a or 4b, page 5)*. It may be helpful to also place a marker in each chain as it is made. This will help you see where to insert your hook on Row 1 *(Fig. 7b, page 7)*.

Foundation Chain: Working across top loops of the ribbon yarn, skip first 4 loops from end and insert hook in next loop, (skip next loop, ch 1) 6 times: 6 chs.

Work all sc using 2 loops *(Figs. 8a & b, page 7)*.

Remove the marker as you work into the marked stitch.

Row 1: Turn; skip first ch, sc in next ch, place marker in sc just made, sc in last 4 chs: 5 sc.

Row 2: Ch 1, turn; skip turning ch just made, sc in next sc, place marker in sc just made, sc in last 4 sc.

Repeat Row 2 until there are at least 4 top loops remaining on the ribbon yarn after completing a row.

Trim the ribbon yarn leaving 4 loops. Secure the loop on hook and hide the raw edge of the ribbon yarn ends *(see Finishing, page 9)*.

The model was made using *Red Heart® Boutique Ribbons®*, #1939 Marble.

INSTRUCTIONS

With Medium Weight yarn, ch 26.

Row 1: Beginning in fourth ch from hook, dc2tog twice **(3 skipped chs count as first dc)**, dc in next 16 chs, 2 dc in each of next 2 chs, dc in last ch, drop yarn: 24 dc.

Working 2 rows with ribbon yarn forms a row of ruffles on each side of the scarf.

When working with ribbon yarn, work all sc using 2 loops *(Figs. 8a & b, page 7)*.

Row 2: Working across top loops of the ribbon yarn, skip first 4 loops from end, insert hook in next loop and pull through loop on hook, turn; sc in each dc across.

Row 3: Ch 1, turn; skip turning ch just made, sc in each sc across; cut ribbon yarn leaving 4 loops.

Row 4: With Medium Weight yarn, ch 3 **(counts as first dc, now and throughout)**, turn; 2 dc in each of next 2 sts, dc in next 16 sts, dc2tog twice, dc in last st.

Row 5: Ch 3, turn; dc2tog twice, dc in next 16 dc, 2 dc in each of next 2 dc, dc in last dc.

Rows 6 and 7: Repeat Rows 4 and 5; at end of Row 7, drop yarn.

Rows 8-82: Repeat Rows 2-7, 12 times; then repeat Rows 2-4 once **more**.

Finish off.

Hide the raw edge of the ribbon yarn ends and weave in all medium weight yarn ends *(see Finishing, page 9)*.

BUTTONED NECK WARMER

 EASY

Shown on page 21.

Finished Size: 4½" x 23¼" (11.5 cm x 59 cm)

SHOPPING LIST

Yarn
(Ribbon Super Bulky Weight)
[3.5 ounces, 42 yards
(100 grams, 38 meters)
per hank]:
☐ 1 hank
(Medium Weight)
[7 ounces, 370 yards
(198 grams, 338 meters) per
skein]:
☐ 1 skein

Crochet Hook
☐ Size I (5.5 mm)
   or size needed for gauge

Additional Supplies
☐ Yarn needle
☐ Sewing needle and
   matching thread
☐ ³/₄" (19 mm) Buttons - 2

GAUGE INFORMATION
With Medium Weight Yarn,
   in pattern,
   12 dc = 4" (10 cm);
   4 rows = 2" (5 cm)
Gauge Swatch: 4"w x 2½"h
   (10 cm x 6.25 cm)
With Medium Weight Yarn, ch 13.
Work same as Neck Warmer
Rows 1-5: 12 dc.
Finish off.

INSTRUCTIONS
With Medium Weight yarn, ch 71.

Row 1: Sc in second ch from hook
and in each ch across: 70 sc.

Row 2: Ch 3 (**counts as first dc,
now and throughout**), turn; (2 dc
in next sc, skip next sc) across
to last sc, dc in last sc: 34 2-dc
groups.

19

Rows 3-7: Ch 3, turn; work 2 dc in center sp of each 2-dc group *(Fig. 13)* across to last dc, dc in last dc.

Cut yarn.

Fig. 13

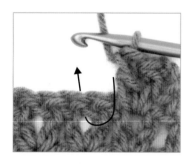

When working with ribbon yarn, work all sc using 2 loops *(Figs. 8a & b, page 7)*.

Row 8: Working across top loops of the ribbon yarn, skip first 4 loops from end, insert hook in next loop and pull through loop on hook, turn; skip turning ch just made, sc in each dc across: 70 sc.

Rows 9 and 10: Ch 1, turn; skip turning ch just made, sc in each sc across.

Cut the ribbon yarn leaving 4 loops. Secure the loop on hook and hide the raw edge of the ribbon yarn ends and weave in all medium weight yarn ends *(see Finishing, page 9)*.

Sew 2 buttons to Row 6, 4 dc from the edge and 4 dc apart. Use spaces between dc on short edge at opposite end for buttonholes.

The model was made using *Red Heart® Boutique Ribbons®*, #1938 City and *Red Heart® With Love®*, #1012 Black.

CHEVRON SCARF

◼◼◻◻ EASY

Finished Size: 7" x 70" (18 cm x 178 cm)

SHOPPING LIST

Yarn
(Ribbon Super Bulky Weight)
[3.5 ounces, 42 yards **SUPER BULKY 6**
(100 grams, 38 meters)
per hank]:
- ☐ 1 hank

(Medium Weight) **MEDIUM 4**
[7 ounces, 364 yards
(198 grams, 333 meters) per
skein]:
- ☐ Color A - 1 skein
- ☐ Color B - 1 skein
- ☐ Color C - 1 skein

Crochet Hook
- ☐ Size I (5.5 mm)
  or size needed for gauge

Additional Supplies
- ☐ Yarn needle
- ☐ Sewing needle and
  matching thread

GAUGE INFORMATION

With Medium Weight Yarn,
in pattern,
2 repeats (28 dc) = 8¹/₄" (21 cm)
Gauge Swatch: 8¹/₄"w x 2¹/₂"h
(21 cm x 6.25 cm)
With Color A, ch 31.
Row 1: Dc in fourth ch from hook
(3 skipped chs count as first dc)
and in next 5 chs, skip next 2 chs,
dc in next 5 chs, 2 dc in each of
next 2 chs, dc in next 5 chs, skip
next 2 chs, dc in next 5 chs, 2 dc in
last ch: 28 dc.
Rows 2-4: Ch 3 **(counts as first dc)**,
turn; dc in first 6 dc, skip next 2 dc,
dc in next 5 dc, 2 dc in each of next
2 dc, dc in next 5 dc, skip next 2 dc,
dc in next 5 dc, 2 dc in last dc.
Finish off.

The model was made using **Red Heart® Boutique Ribbons®**,
#1930 Aurora and **Red Heart® Super Saver®**, #0358 Lavender,
#0776 Dark Orchid, and #0718 Shocking Pink.

🎥CHANGING COLORS

YO, insert hook in last dc, YO and pull up a loop, YO and draw through 2 loops on hook, drop yarn; with new yarn, YO and draw through 2 loops on hook *(Fig. 14)*.

Fig. 14

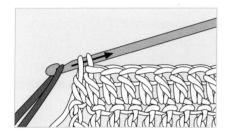

INSTRUCTIONS

With Color A, ch 241.

Row 1: Dc in fourth ch from hook **(3 skipped chs count as first dc)** and in next 5 chs, skip next 2 chs, dc in next 5 chs, ★ 2 dc in each of next 2 chs, dc in next 5 chs, skip next 2 chs, dc in next 5 chs; repeat from ★ across to last ch, 2 dc in last ch: 238 dc.

Row 2: Ch 3 **(counts as first dc, now and throughout)**, turn; dc in first 6 dc, skip next 2 dc, dc in next 5 dc, ★ 2 dc in each of next 2 dc, dc in next 5 dc, skip next 2 dc, dc in next 5 dc; repeat from ★ across to last dc, 2 dc in last dc changing to Color B, cut Color A.

Row 3: Ch 3, turn; dc in first 6 dc, skip next 2 dc, dc in next 5 dc, ★ 2 dc in each of next 2 dc, dc in next 5 dc, skip next 2 dc, dc in next 5 dc; repeat from ★ across to last dc, 2 dc in last dc.

Row 4: Repeat Row 2, changing to Color C in last dc, cut Color B.

Row 5: Repeat Row 3; drop Color C.

Working Rows 6 and 7 with ribbon yarn forms a row of ruffles on each side of the scarf.

When working with ribbon yarn, work all sc using 2 loops *(Figs. 8a & b, page 7)*.

Row 6: Working across top loops of the ribbon yarn, skip first 4 loops from end, insert hook in next loop and pull through loop on hook, turn; skip turning ch just made, sc in each dc across.

Row 7: Ch 1, turn; skip turning ch just made, sc in each sc across; cut ribbon yarn leaving 4 loops.

Row 8: With Color C, repeat Row 2, changing to Color B in last dc, cut Color C.

Row 9: Repeat Row 3.

Row 10: Repeat Row 2, changing to Color A in last dc; cut Color B.

Rows 11 and 12: Repeat Row 3 twice.

Finish off.

Hide the raw edge of the ribbon yarn ends and weave in all medium weight yarn ends *(see Finishing, page 9)*.

Row 2: Ch 1, turn; sc in first 5 sc, ch 3, skip next sc, sc in next 6 sc, ch 3, skip next sc, sc in last 5 sc: 16 sc and 2 ch-3 sps.

Row 3: Ch 3 (**counts as first dc**), turn; dc in next 3 sc, ★ ch 2, skip next sc, sc in next ch-3 sp, ch 2, skip next sc, dc in next 4 sc; repeat from ★ once **more**: 14 sts and 4 ch-2 sps.

Row 4: Ch 1, turn; sc in first 4 dc, ★ sc in next ch-2 sp, ch 3, sc in next ch-2 sp and in next 4 dc; repeat from ★ once **more**: 16 sc and 2 ch-3 sps.

Repeat Rows 3 and 4 for pattern until Scarf measures approximately 39½" (100.5 cm) from beginning ch, ending by working Row 3.

Next Row: Ch 1, turn; sc in first 4 dc, ★ sc in next ch-2 sp, ch 1, sc in next ch-2 sp and in next 4 dc; repeat from ★ once **more**: 16 sc and 2 ch-1 sps.

Last Row: Ch 1, turn; sc in each sc and in each ch-1 sp across; finish off: 18 sc.

RUFFLE

When using mesh yarn, work all sc using 4 loops (**Figs. 9a & b, page 8**).

Row 1: With **wrong** side of last row of Scarf facing, insert hook in first sc, skip first 4 loops on mesh yarn, insert hook in next loop and pull it through sc (**Fig. 10, page 8**), ch 1, skip ch just made, sc in same st and in next sc, (skip next sc, sc in next sc) across: 10 sc.

Rows 2-12: Ch 1, turn; skip turning ch just made, sc in each sc across.

Cut the mesh yarn leaving 4 loops. Secure the loop on hook and hide the raw edge of the mesh yarn ends *(see Finishing, page 9).*

With **wrong** side of opposite end facing and  working in free loops of beginning ch *(Fig. 15)*, **work in same manner as first end.**

Fig. 15

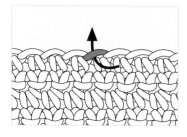

Weave in medium weight yarn ends.

Rnd 2: Ch 5 **(counts as first dc plus ch 2)**, 2 dc in same st, dc in next 2 dc, ★ (2 dc, ch 2, 2 dc) in next dc, dc in next 2 dc; repeat from ★ around, dc in same dc as first dc; join with slip st to first dc, place loop from hook onto safety pin to keep piece from unraveling while working next rnd, drop yarn: 24 dc and 4 ch-2 sps.

When working with mesh yarn, work all sc using 2 loops **(Figs. 8a & b, page 7)**.

Rnd 3: Holding Square with **wrong** side facing and yarn loop out of the way, insert hook in slip st just made; holding mesh yarn **behind** Square and working across top loops, skip first 4 loops from end and insert hook in next loop **(Fig. 16)**, pull loop through st, ch 1, skip ch just made, sc in same st and in next 5 dc, ch 2, (sc in next 6 dc, ch 2) 3 times; working **behind** yarn loop, join with slip st to first sc **(Fig. 10, page 8)**, cut mesh yarn leaving 4 loops.

Fig. 16

Rnd 4: Remove the loop from the safety pin and place it on the hook, then pull it through the mesh yarn loop on hook, ch 3, turn; working **behind** Rnd 3, (dc, ch 2, 2 dc) in first ch-2 sp on Rnd 2, dc in next 6 sc on Rnd 3, ★ (2 dc, ch 2, 2 dc) in next ch-2 sp on Rnd 2, dc in next 6 sc on Rnd 3; repeat from ★ around; join with slip st to first dc, finish off: 40 dc and 4 ch-2 sps.

SQUARE WITH BUTTONHOLE BAND

Work same as Square, but do **not** finish off at end of Rnd 4.

BUTTONHOLE BAND

Row 1: Slip st in next dc and in next ch-2 sp, ch 3, dc in next 10 dc and in next ch-2 sp, leave remaining sts unworked: 12 dc.

Row 2: Ch 1, turn; sc in first 3 dc, ch 2, skip next dc, sc in next 4 dc, ch 2, skip next dc, sc in last 3 dc: 10 sc and 2 ch-2 sps.

Row 3: Ch 3, turn; dc in next sc and in each sc and each ch-2 sp across; finish off.

SQUARE WITH BUTTON BAND

Work same as Square, but do **not** finish off at end of Rnd 4.

BUTTON BAND

Row 1: Slip st in next dc and in next ch-2 sp, ch 3, dc in next 10 dc and in next ch-2 sp, leave remaining sts unworked: 12 dc.

Row 2: Ch 1, turn; sc in each dc across.

Row 3: Ch 3, turn; dc in next sc and in each sc across; finish off.

Pull both mesh yarn ends on each Square to the **wrong** side. Using sewing needle and thread, gather the ends and sew them in place *(see Finishing, page 9).*

Sew buttons to Row 2 of Button Band, placing one in fourth sc from each edge.

Sew Squares together to form a strip, placing a Square with a Band at each end.

Weave in medium weight yarn ends.

Rnd 1 (Wrong side)**:** Change to smaller size hook and stretch the mesh yarn out to work in top loops. Ch 1 using next available top mesh loop *(Fig. 17a)*, place marker in ch just made, 🎥 work 5 sc in top loop of third ch from hook *(Fig. 17b)*. The overlays on Figs. 17b & d are to help you see the top of the stitches.

Rotate Flower placing mesh yarn in **back** and hook in **front** of piece to begin working on opposite side of ch just worked into *(Fig. 17c)*. Work 5 sc in free loop of same ch *(Fig. 17d)*; join with slip st to marked ch, remove marker: 10 sc.

Fig. 17a

Fig. 17c

Fig. 17b

Fig. 17d

Rnd 2: Ch 1, place marker in ch just made, work 2 sc in each of first 5 sc; placing mesh yarn in **back** and hook in **front** of piece, work 2 sc in each of last 5 sc; join with slip st to marked ch, remove marker: 20 sc.

Right Side

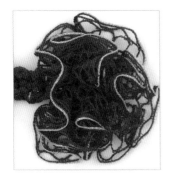

Wrong Side

BAND

Row 1: Change to larger size hook and holding the whole strand of mesh yarn together, ch 1, do **not** turn; sc in first 2 sc, leave remaining sc unworked.

Rows 2-4: Ch 1, turn; sc in each sc.

Row 5: Ch 1, turn; skip first sc, sc in last sc, ch 2.

Work a Flower, work (Band, Flower) 12 times: 14 Flowers.

Cut the mesh yarn leaving 4 loops. Secure the loop on hook and hide the raw edge of the mesh yarn ends *(see Finishing, page 9)*.

INSTRUCTIONS
BUTTON LOOP & CORD

Using larger size hook and holding the whole strand of mesh yarn together, ch 5; join with slip st to form the button loop. Ch 4 for the cord.

FLOWER

When making the Flower, work sc using 2 loops *(Figs. 8a & b, page 7)*.

Rnd 1 (Wrong side)**:** Change to smaller size hook and stretch the mesh yarn out to work in top loops. Ch 1 using next available top mesh loop *(Fig. 17a, page 36)*, place marker in ch just made, work 5 sc in top loop of third ch from hook *(Fig. 17b, page 36)*.

Rotate Flower placing mesh yarn in **back** and hook in **front** of piece to begin working on opposite side of ch just worked into *(Fig. 17c, page 36)*. Work 5 sc in free loop of same ch *(Fig. 17d, page 36)*; join with slip st to marked ch *(Fig. 10, page 8)*, remove marker: 10 sc.

Rnd 2: Ch 1, place marker in ch just made, work 2 sc in each of first 5 sc; placing mesh yarn in **back** and hook in **front** of piece, work 2 sc in each of last 5 sc; join with slip st to marked ch, remove marker: 20 sc.

Right Side

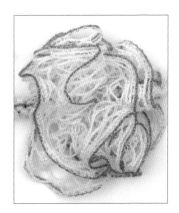

Wrong Side

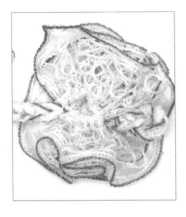

BUTTON CORD

Change to larger size hook and holding the whole strand of mesh yarn together, ch 4, slip st in third ch from hook; finish off leaving 4 loops.

Hide the raw edge of the mesh yarn ends *(see Finishing, page 9).*

Sew a button to the end of the Button Cord.

CORD

Change to larger size hook and holding the whole strand of mesh yarn together, ch 6.

SIZE SMALL ONLY
Work a Flower, work (Cord, Flower) 3 times: 5 Flowers.

SIZE LARGE ONLY
Work a Flower, work (Cord, Flower) 4 times: 6 Flowers.

LONG RUFFLED COWL

 EASY

Finished Size: Approximately 3½" x 50" (9 cm x 127 cm) relaxed

SHOPPING LIST

Yarn
(Mesh Super Bulky Weight)
[3.5 ounces, 20 yards
(100 grams, 18 meters)
per hank]:
- [ ] 2 hanks

Crochet Hook
- [ ] Size I (5.5 mm)

Additional Supplies
- [ ] Sewing needle and matching thread
- [ ] Split ring markers

Gauge is not important for this project.

INSTRUCTIONS

When working a Foundation Chain, place a marker in the first chain made *(Fig. 4a or 4b, page 5)*. It may be helpful to also place a marker in each chain as it is made. This will help you see where to insert your hook on Row 1 *(Fig. 7b, page 7)*.

As you work, stretch the yarn out, having the mesh edge at the top. Work only in the top row of mesh loops.

Foundation Chain: Skip first 8 loops from end and insert hook in next loop, ch 8 without skipping loops between chs.

Instructions continued on page 46.

The model was made using *Red Heart® Boutique Sashay Sequins™*, #1948 Mediterranean.

SHORT COWL

 EASY

Finished Size: Approximately 4" x 30" (10 cm x 76 cm) circumference

Gauge is not important for this
project.

INSTRUCTIONS

When working a Foundation
Chain, place a marker in the first
chain made (*Fig. 4a or 4b, page 5*).
It may be helpful to also place a
marker in each chain as it is made.
This will help you see where
to insert your hook on Row 1
(*Fig. 7b, page 7*).

Foundation Chain: Working
across top loops of the ribbon
yarn, skip first 4 loops from end,
insert hook in next loop, ch 16
without skipping loops between
chs.

Work all sc using 2 loops (*Figs. 8a
& b, page 7*).

Remove the marker as you work
into the marked stitch.

The model was made using
Red Heart® Boutique Ribbons®, #1941 Rosebud.

Continued from page 44.

Row 1: Turn; skip first ch, sc in next ch, place marker in sc just made, sc in last 14 chs: 15 sc.

Row 2: Ch 1, turn; skip turning ch just made, sc in next sc, place marker in sc just made, sc in last 14 sc.

Repeat Row 2 until Cowl measures approximately 30" (76 cm) from Foundation Ch.

Cut the ribbon yarn leaving 4 loops. Secure the loop on hook *(see Finishing, page 9)*. Twist the Cowl once and using sewing needle and thread, sew the ends together.

LONG RUFFLED COWL

Continued from page 43.

Work all sc using 4 loops *(Figs. 9a & b, page 8)*.

Remove the marker as you work into the marked stitch.

Row 1: Turn; skip first ch, sc in next ch, place marker in sc just made, sc in last 6 chs: 7 sc.

Row 2: Ch 1, turn; skip turning ch just made, sc in next sc, place marker in sc just made, sc in last 6 sc.

Repeat Row 2 until Cowl measures approximately 50" (127 cm) from Foundation Ch.

Cut the mesh yarn leaving 8 loops. Secure the loop on hook *(see Finishing, page 9)*. Using sewing needle and thread and making sure the Cowl is not twisted, sew the ends together.

GENERAL INSTRUCTIONS

ABBREVIATIONS

ch	chain(s)
cm	centimeters
dc	double crochet(s)
dc2tog	double crochet 2 together
mm	millimeters
Rnd(s)	Round(s)
sc	single crochet(s)
sp(s)	space(s)
st(s)	stitch(es)
YO	yarn over

SYMBOLS & TERMS

★ — work instructions following ★ as many **more** times as indicated in addition to the first time.

( ) or [ ] — work enclosed instructions **as many** times as specified by the number immediately following **or** work all enclosed instructions in the stitch or space indicated **or** contains explanatory remarks.

colon (:) — the number(s) given after a colon at the end of a row or round denote(s) the number of stitches or spaces you should have on that row or round.

GAUGE

Exact gauge is essential for proper size. Before beginning your project, make the sample swatch given in the individual instructions in the yarn and hook specified. After completing the swatch, measure it, counting your stitches and rows carefully. If your swatch is larger or smaller than specified, make another, changing hook size to get the correct gauge. **Keep trying until you find the size hook that will give you the specified gauge.**